WINTER
READY

T0159405

ALSO BY LELAND KINSEY

Winter Ready

The Immigrant's Contract

In the Rain Shadow

Sledding on Hospital Hill

Not One Man's Work

Family Drives

Northern Almanac

WINTER READY

poems

❧

LELAND KINSEY

GREEN WRITERS PRESS   *Brattleboro, Vermont*

Printed in the United States

10 9 8 7 6 5 4 3 2 1

Giving Voice to Writers Who Will Make the World a Better Place
Green Writers Press | Brattleboro, Vermont
www.greenwriterspress.com

ISBN: 978-0-9899838-4-6

Green Writers Press gratefully acknowledges support
from individual donors, friends, and readers to help
support the environment and our publishing initiative.

COVER PHOTO BY THE AUTHOR
WITH AN ANTIQUE BELLOWS CAMERA

PRINTED IN VERMONT AT A FAMILY-OWNED PRINTER ON PAPER
WITH PULP THAT COMES FROM FSC-CERTIFIED FORESTS, MANAGED
FORESTS THAT GUARANTEE RESPONSIBLE ENVIRONMENTAL, SOCIAL,
AND ECONOMIC PRACTICES. MADE WITH A CHLORINE-FREEPROCESS
(ECF: ELEMENTAL CHLORINE FREE).

CONTENTS

∾

WINTER
READY

POINTING THE CHIMNEY

I climbed to the three-story rooftop
of my house; tried to keep
my balance on the ladder hung
by rope from the old antenna base
left standing like a ship's busted spar.

With the ogee of the trowel blade
I pushed the stiff mortar far
into the crevices from which old mortar had fallen
both onto the roof and ground, and down
inside the unlined flue.

In places I could see completely through
to that darkening well of light
more than four stories tall
from the basement floor.

When I'd opened the ash-pit door
and begun the annual cleaning,
I'd noticed pieces of grout clinking
against the shovel amidst the soot
and creosote debris. To keep
the chimney from going to wrack

I carefully pointed and packed
each crevice, bed joint, head joint,

between course after course of common bond,
tucking carefully by flashing and cricket.
I scraped mortar from the board
until it lay even with each stretcher's face.

After it dries for a time, I'll place
the trowel's curved edge against
each grout line; using it as a float,
I'll run it hard for a concave finish.

The lime in the concrete will not diminish
the strength too greatly. Without it
the mortar would be much harder
than the old bricks and its expansion
would cause them to fracture or spall.

I'll be careful not to let anything fall,
or me, from my odd high perch,
when I finally climb to mould a crowning rim
of wire-reinforced grout daub by daub,
my awkward form
bent to the day's work.

CHIMNEY SWIFTS

Pointing the chimney,
I startled, almost off the roof.
Up shot from the flue's mouth
like shrapnel from a mortar
flew dozens of swifts,
and flew higher like flinders
from an exploding shell.
Once the optical illusion
          of their alternate wing beats
ceased, they soared,
          their tight cigar-like bodies
and boomerang wings
          whirling in outside loops,
Immelmann turns, stalls,
          nosedives, hunting
and eating on the fly.
Then, since they cannot perch,
ignoring me
they dove like dropped stones
back down the flue's mouth,
but en masse looked like smoke returning,
to where I could not see them
in the dark well.
          I could hear
the scratching of their small claws
and bristly bracing tails; the small sound
and tiny echo of their twittering calls.

I have sometimes found a nestling
in the ashes, fallen,
and no way to replace it.

But these were postbreeders
in some numbers
colonizing my creosote-
stained, cold-spalled chimney
that I'm trying to keep standing.
The birds will migrate soon
from this narrow room,
this edifice I serve
which serves us well.
I'll clean the hard and the ashy
residues of last year's fires.
The stiff brushes for this work
will also scrape away
the few spit and twig crescents
that, like fragile boats, floated
their seasonal, small-white-egg
and nestling cargo
over depths the living
never plumbed.

PLAYING FUNGO

My grown son asks to go out
and have me hit a few
before first snow. I lay down
hard grounders and shout
"Good stop." His way
of staying connected to his youth,
not distant, and me.

I remember a time
I could swing the bat with ease,
no hitch in the hips,
back muscles wouldn't seize.
The days stretched long
for my brother and me, in sharp-
stubble fields as we got so good
we were so far apart
we could hardly talk;
or with the few neighbor kids,
for inning after uncounted inning.

Grass wore out, and stained.
Dirt scrapes, close calls--self called—
gave one a sense of winning
even when the score was lopsided,
as were the poorly made balls
when ash and hide cracked
for hit, foul, or out.

When horsehide and cowhide collided
on pitches or plays in the field,
the odor of leather

and the neatsfoot oil we rubbed
into the gloves all winter
rose like a mist,
rose like the mist
from warm ground late evenings
that you could lose your ball in
when we couldn't decide
how to yield.

       Or like the heavier fog
.burning off fall mornings
when the season and season
were ending, and our longest throws
and deepest drives had rhythm
and no reason.

WINTER READY

I walked through bottle gentian, asters, nettles,
last blooms of the late bloomers
in this cold northern peat bog.
The cotton grass stood with tops tipped
like half-picked bolls. I gathered one
and rolled it between my fingers,
like unpacking a milkweed pod,
but only the husks of those remain.
The sedges of the swamp had frosted beige,
and the leaves of Labrador tea hung grey
like the drying fish on clotheslines
I saw in the Shetlands, or as if someone
had trapped the lemmings present
and was drying their coarse-haired skins.
A few bees, golden northerns and red tails
still bumbled among the flowers,
along with virescent green metallics,
all soon to die but for young mated females
who will ensconce themselves in soil chambers
in the swamp's firmer edges and cut banks.
                         I'd seen the bees first
in late April, when frost still lay in early morning
and ice had retreated only a little
in the channel and the pond. They'd been on
blooming bog rosemary, and leatherleaf.
The wood frogs, now sunk deep in mud,
then gurgled their breeding-season song,
making a watery world seem even more liquid.
Tree sparrows, now months gone, were already dimpling
the surface with their dives for early insects
amongst the small flocks of ducks and grebes

waiting for wider play to nest and lay
the eggs whose progeny swim now
with adults in large rafts on the peaty water.
A raft of mergansers seemed to organize a herding
as they spread out and noisily displayed,
moving toward a rocky shallows
where they feasted on small fish driven before them.
They would have had a much wider way
a few thousand years ago in the ongoing
recovery from the glacial plowing
of this whole part of the world
to bare rock, gravel wash,
and snaking eskers.
                              A broken
buried block melted to a shallow lake
in this valley. Plants like leatherleaf returned,
growing in mats
                        and so hardy
that they became the base for spagnums—
now autumn red and yellow across the bog—
which rot and float; support more growth
in the acidifying swamp;
in turn grow thick enough to hold up shrubs
like the Labrador tea, mountain fly honeysuckle,
rhodora, lambskill, all desiccated now
as I stood among them, all trembling
as I walked the quaking mire.
I passed large cedar roots
that had taken hold before they were sawn
for squirt dams at the outlet,
a narrow boulder-strewn throat
still crossed with rusted cable.
Large rock-embedded eye bolts

remain where loggers boomed logs
across the flooded swamp from winter landings
ready for the spring ice out
when they sluiced them through
the knocked out raceway.
     The yearly drowning
drove the encroaching forest back for a time;
small cedars drowned, their stumps now stand
    like weathered fence posts
in drooping lines failing to hold
     anything in or out.

The resident harrier circled—spruce and cedar
growth narrow his prime hunting grounds,
succession, eutrophication–
ready to stoop on vole or deer mouse,
or rarer lemming, whose ancestors were ice-pushed
this far south and farther.
I found
seed piles, cranberry, teaberry, bearberry
by the mouths of rodent runs.
Caribou moss punched up
in tight fists among the sedges
though caribou haven't fed on it for millennia.
  But a sudden uprise and wake
from the channel announced a bull moose
who'd been feeding entirely underwater.
His wide rack carried water lily
and spatterdock stems, leaves,
and leathery berries, which also draped
across his long humped back,
he and they a dripping mass
as his feet found purchase

and he lumbered off, mouth full
of arrowhead root the Indians
called duck potatoes,
for which they would open
muskrats' dens to take the rodent's caches.
　　Muskrat houses and feeding
platforms dotted the swamp, bitten
reed and rush debris floating free.
Beavers, extirpated long ago,
now returning to the tributary headwaters,
had loosed the odd food stick
from underwater, weighted piles.
I saw them swifting along
the channel and pond in the wind.
　　That wind will hone
to a fine edge in the months to come,
or swirl great snow devils
down the buried bog's length.
I noted the occasional leatherwood
shrub in case I need to peel one
in my winter treks, to use the impossibly
resilient bark as repairing thong
for snowshoe or toboggan lash.
I've had to work my way alone before
and still decline to be at the end
of any electronic leash, though
signals here would be distant and poor.
　　When I return in mid-winter
to go owling at night, calling them in
to photograph, hearing the saw whet's
metallic call that would have reminded
any sleepy sawyer of his evening chore,
or the long eared's most owl-like hooh,

I will find out if tactics
and stores of animals and plants
have been sufficient to get them through.

Everything that does not migrate
has fattened up, bedded down,
cocooned up, seeded itself.
Life's two principles—
reproduce; survive to reproduce again.
By this process the world is brought
back to us as we know at winter's end.
And by this process, even beyond
the evident hand of man, the world
slowly changes utterly.

CIDER

Apples, drops, and those shaken, star the ground
in dense constellations. Star colors too,
from yellow to deep red,
but also Lubsk Queen's pure porcelain,
like white dwarfs, and permain's blue cast,
like the hottest. All lie cold.
The day lies grand, but mid-fall,
as I gather bag after bag that sag
over my shoulders as I lug them.
I load so many I wish I had a cider mill
where the crushed apples were tossed
on a floor that was jacked apiece
to press against the building's resistant frame
and reinforced planked ceiling
and rivers of cider would run to vats below.
I have only a hand-built hopper
with a nail studded cylinder to grate
these apples to bits as I pour
them in peck by peck,
the motor loading, the wheel gnashing
little explosions of juice and apple parts.
                    My press itself
is an old plywood press from the defunct
veneer mill with a hand-turn screw
I work with a four foot wrench.
The pomace is stacked, wrapped pad
by layered cheesecloth pad
in a slotted hardwood frame
I sawed the pieces for from rock maple
and screwed together to stand
the strain.

Each squeeze
is a ten to fifteen gallon run
strained bottle by bottle
through additional cheesecloth.
After I have expressed all I can,
I must lift each hefty packet
of damp pomace and empty
it into the barrow to be wheeled
to the hornet- and wasp-encircled waste pile.
By the end I am drenched
and flooded from the cider rain.

DOUBLE DIGGING THE GARDEN

The first shovel depth turns easily,
a fine built-loam of native soil,
and the manure, leaves, wood stove cinders,
garden debris, kitchen garbage,
that heat of their own accord
at the middle of the compost pile
and burn to a fine grey ash,
which I forked steaming in the late fall air
into the wheelbarrow to spread
on the plot before I began my tilth.
I build a berm as I spade the first trench.

The second shovel depth is hard to turn,
a remnant of the glacial till
pushed by ice and dropped as heavy sediment
in the great plowing of this region.
But I want some clay in my topsoil
and a deeper richness in the bed
to hold water and nourish
in summer drought.

I want crops like my uncle's field corn
that once stood fourteen foot;
French white radishes like baseballs;
enough cucumbers for four kinds of pickles
plus relish; tomatoes for sauce, juice,
piccalilli, and eating out of hand;
lettuces like thick knots making up a variegated
carpet in hues from greens to reds.

My wife and I now have way too much

of all of this. Our children are gone.
Pets, large and small, which used to consume the extra
have long since died. I squeeze, can, freeze,
dry. My grandmother had jars of raspberries
dated a decade old, and I may soon match
that mark with many supplies.
I give much away; will have to give more,
to extended family, neighbors, food banks.
I could join the farmer's market
but don't like meeting new people.
My legacy may consist of refuse.

By the turn of mid-afternoon my spine
feels bent and raised like the spade's frog.
For two brisk days, heated by work,
I fill the ditch just dug with the diggings
of the new all the way to the end of my tillage,
then barrow the levee at the start down
to fill the last.
        The soil lies loose, aerated,
and free of any rocks the deep frost forced up.
It will drain and open easily in spring
for cold-hardy crops, and warm quickly
for fainter seeds.

Each summer I bring friends out
to note and share the display and produce.
Here is life's habit on grand exhibit
and the hard work hidden.

FALL LIGHT

The light in my dining room turns golden
for two weeks each fall.
                    I sit, read, and write
in that room at that time of year.
A north-facing room usually slightly
blue in tone, even when sun comes in
under the porch roof and through the side window
early mornings.
The tree's color does not rivet one,
not the deep reds, various oranges,
or the purples of the most striking trees,
or especially those with variegated leaves,
but draws attention nonetheless.
For a time the tree stands a stately yellow,
like the sun at height
if you could look at it, and that is the light
the tree reflects and diffuses into my room
through the huge leaded picture window
the original housewrights thought to put
looking out on the town thoroughfare.
The sun, in its southern sphere now,
hits the tree full on.
                  Nothing much going on
in the street beyond the hedge, this quiet
part of the world's bustle now in the tall maple's shadow.
But in here, illumination a painter might die for,
a photographer would use filters to achieve,
and which in cinema would be memory itself.

The several million leaves,
unnoticed each by each, fall,

after they shine and fade
like individual frames in this part
of the movie we call *Days,*
till the last one passes from the light
into the rolling dark.

UPLAND BIRDS

Treading on mast and leaf litter
I came to the edge of a sharp uprise
over which rose the head and shoulders
of the biggest black bear I'd ever seen.
He threw his front paws up
as if being arrested
and half threw himself half fell
back down the slope
on which partridge- and wintergreen berries
grew, but I doubted they were fruits
for his labors, and at the bottom
went galumphing off,
the fat of his sides visibly jiggling.
I could see criss-crossed claw marks
on the bark of beeches, runic-like tales
of cubs' escape from danger,
the male I just watched disappear
perhaps included, if they weren't his.

I'd stood atop a similar ledgy rise
and had a grouse burst in full flight
through the tops of the trees.
I stood above then beside it,
and felt its air-wake wash
my face as an even faster goshawk
raced across the same small open space
so close I heard the soft crick-creak
a hawk or falcons wings will make at full tilt,
and foolishly felt sorry for the grouse
which I would have shot if I'd been quicker.

All day I heard the muffled thumps
like the tumble and thuds
of my grandfather starting
his old John Deere tractor,
or heard it only after I felt
the low-pitched drumming,
of a grouse beating his wings before him
like cupped hands clapping.
I thought I knew the wolf tree log,
the hollow butt-end left by loggers,
he might be displaying on.
When close I only walked while he beat,
and at the last he took off
with a similar sound
from the great tree's rotting bole,
and amidst his thunder my own
ended his lovely trouble.
The day produced two other offerings.
I shot one grouse's head off as it peeked
from behind a beech
where it was feeding on the burry nuts
layered in among the leaves
of the main tree and many seedlings
growing in their plot they poison
the ground of to hold. I waited
for the rustle of leaves to end
before approach and almost lost
the bird as it blended with the forest floor.
It warmed my hand
As I thrust it in my game bag.
The other shuddered up
from where I could have tripped on it,

and put me on my heels.
I said aloud after it, "Good job,"
as it skirted behind cover.
I saw no more of them,
but others' distant drumming
thrummed in my own breastbone.

THE SPAWNING HOLE

Because an older friend of his would mention it
but never reveal location,
my friend found the river's major brook trout
spawning hole for at least the second time
by walking the aldery reaches; field meanders;
rocky rapids; and marshy spans;
greenstone and granite defiles
too narrow to fish; boulder-strewn flats;
slate-bedded runs;
sand- and gravel- tailed pools,
over the course of several falls.
One mist-defined October morning
he walked up on the older man
frying two trout beside a lively curve
and race near beaverwork.
"It's taken you a while.
I've cooked one up for you."

Only once or twice a year
do we drift our weighted flies
out beside overgrown banks,
over twig and leaf deposits
heading the clear gravel run.
We quickly land and release
all females; and the largest males,
crook-jawed and shimmering
with muscle and color
giving them the weight
feel and shine of an ingot.
But we keep one or two

medium males apiece
because our families like to eat trout,
and to keep it all from being
just sport.

SWALLOWS

The swallows have left
and it is only August. They gathered
by the thousands on the wires
above the marsh
along the river road.
I yearly wonder where they perched
before rural electrification drove
the transmission works across the swamp
where they roost high-summer nights,
great clouds of them funneling down
among the reeds, then one day
seem to disappear,
and every year so early gone from the marshes
that medieval Europeans imagined
torpid swarms slept the winter
in the ooze beneath the water.
Still their departure is a harbinger
of harbingers.

Only the tree swallow is that in spring,
arriving before most bloom and birth,
chattering calls like any liquid falling,
able to survive the scarcity
of flying insects by eating berries
and beetles for a time,
even dipping water boatmen
from the bath of flood,
rejuvenating flow that would be welcome
in those parts of Mexico
where I saw water boatmen eggs
sold as a kind of caviar,

and watched dried eggs and adults' bodies
being ground for flour.
Tree swallows there wear tattered
mossy coats instead of the sharp metallic green
of their appearance here,
which they've already begun to lose
by the time of their huge pre-roosting,
pre parting, displays.

Like the bank swallows gathering
in post fledging communes,
seeming to fall from the sky
at dusk
on their dusky wings
like sand cascading down
the freshly cut banks they nest in.
My siblings and I would watch
them at the stream-defined
ends of fields, at the embankment
cornices, dropping white feathers—
often those shed by the farm's pigeons—
as mating ritual,
and used for bedding the nests.
 They used to nest in the gravel pit—
long since defunct, dug out,
on my grandmother's land—
high up, just under the fresh lip
whose ragged edge
my brother and I often walked,
and sometimes slipped through
tearing soil, nests, rock, ourselves
in the long slide down,
knowing such vertical excursions

had killed other smart boys
who thought themselves immune.
And how the swallows would dive at us then.

The rough-winged swallows
also nested in the stream banks,
often in burrows kingfishers had
dug the year before,
but not in large numbers.
I'd watch them as I fished
the long black curves
for trout that sought
the same food they did.
Now when I glass them
I can make out the small serrations
on the wing's leading edge
they're named for,
which may create
small mating whistles,
but then they seemed good company
and dull viewing,
though not when gathered
in their vast late-summer congregations.

The cliff swallows I knew then
mostly congregated under barn eaves
and bridge abutments,
hundreds of retort-shaped nests
crowded en masse.
They daubed them up
from rolled mud balls
made on the river fed mud flats
of our glacial valley,

the clayey soil the bank and rough-wings
wouldn't deign to dig in.
The down-turned flask-like mouths
made each nest look
like some ancient amphora
being dumped, as if the barns
were ships keels skyward and their cargo
was spilling.
Spillage occurred.
If one paid close attention
you saw eggs fall as parasitic members
of the clan cleaned out
hosts' nests (the ground
around the foundation looking
like a tempera mural
were being prepared), then each laid
her own egg, or, more remarkably,
would carry an egg in her mouth
to place for raising by others.
The colony was occasionally abandoned,
deaths from the hard summer before,
too much cold or rain
crashing the population,
or infestations too heavy to fight
that a season's sun baking
the empty nests would destroy.
Now the numbers are simply
diminishing.

Barn swallows are also harder
to find, southern sanctuaries
changed or gone.
Those long-passed summers

several pairs would fill our barn
with their blue bolts of action
as we tried to fill it with hay.
Ten thousand bales
we hove into the bays
and piled to the rafters
while the parents tried to raise
and fledge young in the turmoil
and crowding, and they all
mostly escaped before being shut in.
Now only one pair repairs
to my barn each year,
and I fear even they may also be lost.
I damp soil for nest building,
and leave a door open day round
for very early morning feeding.
I daily note the adults bright
flight and conversing,
and try not each time
to think of rescue.
I've often had to catch
young barn swallows
as they thrashed about the horse barn
their wings, or tails, or both
enshrouded by shed-spider webs,
those large orbs woven near every window,
whose light draws the young on first flight
as likely passage, and they tear
the sticky threads till they're dragging
so much silk and encased insects
they cannot fly long
but flutter up and fall
to shelf or floor, but will work hard

to escape a hand
so capture must be quick and sure,
as must the cleaning;
then I carry them out the door
and release them
into the pure light and air
they sought and had been thwarted
by seeking.

IN THE CRANBERRY BOG

The large cranberry plants arch
over the water or close to the run
flowing from beaver dams above
and slowed to a channel
through the sphagnum flats,
which stretch like fields
toward the open water
of the remaining kettle pond.
The peat moss lays purple, orange,
over brush-root hummocks
often topped with small cranberries
like carnelian beads,
but they are not the crop I'm after.

Moose paths, vole and lemming runs,
crisscross the sedgy quaking bog,
which often sinks enough beneath me
so the water almost overtops
my tall boots. At the most quivery
places I gingerly sidestep,
not wanting to break through
to whatever muddy soup,
whatever black-water rooms,
the vegetative mat floats above.

The large cranberries often grow thickest
around greyed cedar stumps
that line the dank banks.
I stoop each by each
and the berries come to hand hazy
but are finger brushed

to a deep plum color
as they rattle into my pail.
Dolls eye berries of dogbane
seem to peer over the scene.
Chewed berries and seeds lay
in piles by rodent nest entrances
to small halls in the drier hummocks.

I've knelt picking, looking close,
like this in Labrador,
where each tiny hillock, moss-topped,
through which dew berries push,
is a small tableau in late August
of a New England round mountain
in mid fall. I'm surrounded
by a number of the latter this gathering day,
but, knees wet, hands cold, senses startled,
I focus on the miniature scene,
and feel delight as large
as if the part were the whole,
as if there were a whole.

CORN CUTTING

I swung the sickle,
doing what used to be fieldwork,
cutting my garden corn.
Ten rows, cutting, stacking,
an hours work;
another hour to feed
them through the shredder
for compost.
Two more hours to turn
out the stubble
so it won't overwinter
borers and fungi.

My grandfather, and those
before, cut whole fields by hand.
Long days bent low
arms going around
a bunch in a row
that could be cut
with one swing
of an oft-honed sickle.
My mother, aunt, and uncles
had been paid a dime
a row to weed the kale
and other weeds smothering
the early seedlings.

A hired man following
tied bundles of stalks
to be wagon gathered.
Later my grandfather rode

on the back seat
of the single head cutter—
at first horse-, then tractor-, drawn—
finishing the knot
in the twine
from the automatic feeder
around the stately gathered corn
on the little steel balcony
before he let each sheaf fall.

He once plucked out a stalk
on which the cob grew
as absolute finial,
and handed it to me,
"Show them at the house."
Carrying it like a battle pennant
much taller than me
I ran from the field
but the speed and wavering
busted the cob
from its base.
I laid them out on the entry floor
ashamed as I told mother
and grandmother to come see
the wonder, and what I had done.
They were amazed and laughed
but I knew my grandfather's prize
was undone.

All the family men,
finally even me,
gathered the corn
and brought it to the chopper

to be cut fine
and blown into the silo.
At first the chopper was run
by a team on the horsepower,
but later steam then gasoline engines
spun the heavy cutter wheel
so fast the paddle blades
also shot
the silage up through
the lofty pipe.
In only a few days
the ensilage juice would pool
around the silo base
and stink like the rankest liquor.

Corn grown this far north
is usually for green chop
not for cobs or kernels
so no hulling combines here,
just multi-headed forage machines
that can reduce
an entire field
in a few hours
to silage blown
into huge harvester wagons
now mostly emptied
into cement sided bunker silos
where it's tractor packed—
a dangerous job
at the high edges—
into dense sustaining winter feed.

Between our place
when I was young

and my grandfather's, ten farms
once ran, poor to prosperous.
One remains.
My cousin has kept
most of the fields in tillage
and farther flung farms
have taken up the remains.
Hired men used to be
unsettled locals; itinerants;
wiry drunks, who slept
in back chambers
ill-heated ells;
mostly they're Mexicans now
trying to live quietly
in a very cold climate,
their living quarter trailers
snow-banked and rusting.
They keep the hours
we used to keep,
running machinery late
on weather-pinched nights,
up early on bracing days.

This day my hand seems curved
from the sickle haft,
my back strong and aching.
The air is filled
with the fine smell
of freshly cut corn,
the crop itself long since harvested,
and all my work seems relic
but of some moment.

WELDING

Before I stored tools
and machines from the winter
onslaught, or need them
in the face of it,
I needed busted draw bars;
broken gears; torn guards,
welded.
    I welded
  on the farm when young,
  parts where neatness
  didn't matter, and heavy
  I-bars made cutting
  through unlikely.

I trundled my damaged goods
to a neighbor who came back
from the WWII,
who'd repaired airplanes
that flew over the Himalayas
from India to China,
the aluminum highway
they called it,
paved by so many crashes
along its length.
He once told how means
to arc weld that metal
had been figured out—
the right alloys and temperatures
for the coated rods.
"Cutting a clean edge
for repairs to flack-blown holes
and storm caused tears

was simple in that light fabric,
but laying down an air-worthy
bead took time to learn,
and when they went down,
and all those god-damned planes
went down, you wondered.
By the time we were through
with the trucks, tractors,
tools, and dollies that carried
and serviced everything
in that rough mess
they all carried half their weight
in weld rod."
The hum
of the transformer
filled his shop
as he bent over
each damaged piece,
which held one welder clamp,
and he held the other
with a rod in its teeth
ready to strike the arc,
and just before that spark
he'd lower the mask
with the black-glass
to protect his eyes
from the incandescence
that will burn holes
in one's retinas.
   I remember striking
   the arc too early,
   the mask still up,
   the blinding flash,
   and the sear on my face.

The mask/arc rhythm
is second nature
to him now,
but he remembers
many times turning in
on those long-ago nights
with swollen
and watery eyes
from passing
the last moment of safety
trying to be sure
of thickness and placement.

The sun going down
in this late season
travels along the horizon,
as if the arc were being struck
to weld the clouds
to the glowing hills,
an obvious image,
and a poor seam
that quickly rends.

He shuts the humming
machine down;
hangs his mask.
I laugh softly.
The beads he laid here
will likely outlast
him, me,
and the machines they mend.

PICKING STONE

—for Jeff

Fifteen acres of upturned soil,
heavily scattered with stones,
that my cousin plowed
to plant this fall, before
his diagnosis of cancer
kept him from the necessary clearing,
lay before us.
I and other family volunteered
for a farm's worst work,
to scrabble over that tillage
picking the rocks, from fist-sized
to those too heavy to lift,
so planting and reaping machinery
would survive.

      We would too,
but faced a hot south wind
that dried the clayey soil to dust
and swirled it into devils
that clogged our noses
and coated our tongues and throats.
We could not drink enough
and knew the next day
we would know the all-body ache
that dry hard work makes.

Gloves could partly protect
fingers and palms from sharp edges
and pinches and raps between stones.
Those we couldn't lift
we slid onto the stone boats,

and lugged plenty almost too big
to make our loads,
dumped at a field-edge embankment
that began to look like an abandoned
weather-dumped wall
made of stone barely stone, like shale
and mudstone; through those forms
laid down, sunk and melted;
to that from the mantle,
long cooled and heavy as the day.

I also knew some one of us likely picked
a rock from the moon,
or Mars, or a leftover bit
from the Solar System's swirling creation,
some stony meteorite,
or carbonaceous chondrite
that likely bore water and acids
as precursors to life. One might notice
the black surface, pitted nature,
or peculiar weight, and still not recognize
what one had in hand. No ceremony then
or now, work bracketed
by beginnings and endings.

My cousin is well enough
to plant the field for cropping
next spring, but he will not live
to cut it for green chop, and knows it.
If only we could reverse it,
the burning up to falling dust.

Last winter wild turkeys came

out of the woods regularly
to feed in his bunker silo.
He poached several,
said it seemed fair, he and the flock
providing each other easy meals.
"They don't need to pick grit
for their gizzards to grind silage,
and the meat's so tender."
He hopes to invite us to such a meal
this early winter.

As I left, he acknowledged
my father's past push to extend tillage
on upland hardscrabble
while my uncle's land laid
that much closer
to the good soil laid down
in the beds of ice age lakes,
        "Well, I know you must love me,
I never thought I'd see *you* pick stone again."

                    Little enough burden.

THE TURKEY BUTCHER

My sister and her husband slaughtered
their turkeys today,
or had them slaughtered.
Nowadays a man traipses
his all-in-one butchering shop
from localvore meat farmer
to localvore meat farmer.

The turkeys were shipped
in early spring
to the town feed store
for designated pick-up days.
The chicks are fragile
and must be under heat lamps
or bare bulbs quickly,
especially in this chill north.
They graduate from warm box
to turkey house before crowding
makes them dangerous
to each other, they'll smother
easily and fast. Free range
once the season's warmer,
they must have cover,
and be herded inside
in a hard rain
or these much diminished fowl
from their wily wild cousins
will often hold their heads up
beak open and drown.
A good fence keeps out skunks
when the chicks are little,

and you can watch
foxes and coyotes pad around
the turkey's whole short life.
Some years top netting
is needed if a hawk or owl
begins feeding.

We entered the pen
of the gobbling rabble
to gather them one by one,
then gently pushed them
head down
into the killing cone
where a carotid is cut
for a quick bleed.
    When I was a boy we pithed
each turkey brain with a knife
through the mouth
to make the bird insensible
and to keep the blood warm
for the slower hand plucking.
My hands remember
the whisper of feathers across them
and the warm pebbled skin.
I would touch my tongue
to the roof of my own mouth
when I heard the bony arch snap
before the blade
like a broken branch.
Today we shackled the legs
into the washer and dipped
the birds into the scalder
so when we dropped them

into the Featherman
the soft rubber fingers
could pluck the feathers easily
as the bodies rapidly spun,
like a massage
on a dangerous fair ride.
The soggy feathers shot
out a back chute as pure waste.
    We children used to gather
the softest from under the pluckers
as replacement for down.

We lifted the clean bodies
to the stainless steel gutting table.
The butcher's deft cuts
first opened the joints
to remove the feet.
He snapped off the head
on the table's edge
but left the esophagus to pull
out the craw;
spun the body around
and sliced open the abdomen
to eviscerate entrails,
lungs, and heart.
    One Sunday dinner, when little,
 I ate the turkey heart
before being told
it was my grandfather's
favorite part.
With a neat cut around
the vent the guts are clear
and never severed.

Into the first chilling
tank they went,
what he called the pink water.
The water in the second tank
sat cold and clear
as a mountain pond
even when he pulled
the last bird from it.
We bagged them in plastic
and ran them quickly
up to the freezer.
      I could carry one plucked bird
as a boy, a grown man two,
as we trundled them
down to sink them
into the refrigerated water
of the milk house cooling tank
that usually held milk cans
for shipping, this before bulk tanks
but after just spring-fed cold.
Toward the end of a long evening
we lugged them back
to the wrapping table.
      I remember the long rolls
of freezer paper at my cousins,
the sizzle and whir of unrolling
before the slap of the carcass
and the crinkle of intricate folds.
I wished I had such reams
to draw on, my trains,
ghost towns, large scale battles
put to paper.
      Into the rust-riddled rattly bed

of a pickup from before the war
we loaded those brown bundles
to be taken to the freezer locker
in town, then sold to buyers
come in on the train.

Today's work took only a morning,
the butcher has another scad
this afternoon.
                    I brought two birds home,
thankful for the gift,
and that the morning was over,
and that I could think of it
with a certain kindness.

READING

I used to read *Farmer Boy* to my boy,
just as my mother read it
to my siblings and me.
But I sit on his bed in bright lamp light.
My mother sat at the top
of the stairs, between bedrooms,
and read by candlelight
and later flashlight,
the wan column of light falling
on each of us when she was done.
The house had been wired
during the war by Rural Electric,
so only the downstairs was done
and poorly. She sometimes sat
in brighter light unseen by us
and played piano for us.
Through the open stairwell door
music flowed, the reverse of cascades,
rose up riser and tread and cold air well
as she played slow jazz, show tunes,
and fast paced hymns.
We slept after our chores
while father and she finished theirs.
I often sang to my son,
work songs from the thirties
or protest songs from my own youth.

The boy in the book knew cold—
driving oxen in deep snow,
cutting ice—
as did we. Water in winter

froze on our dressers,
and the iron stove in the morning
sat like fresh dug Arctic ore.
Woods work for firewood
or logs to sell often chilled
hands and feet beyond feeling,
but, Oh, the ache of its return.
My son's known cold, but not that,
or the purple swelling of frozen ears,
or the agony of chill blains
after outdoor winter work.
But neither did his kinder childhood
allow him to know
the work he did helped pull
the family through.

LEAVES FOR RASPBERRIES

My neighbor is gathering leaves
from all over town in large
appliance boxes, and carting them home
in his ancient Saab. Both he and the car
wheeze at work. He fills the boxes that barely fit
the car; mounds the maple, ash, elm, willow
leaves beside his large raspberry patch;
walks scuffling and kicking with rake in hand
to move the leaves among the canes
to suppress weeds and mimic
their natural domain of forest clearings,
humus. He eases other's work,
and loads it on himself.
He's pruned the canes to four feet tall,
and when the leaves almost top the tips
he calls it quits, except for the dressing
of pine needles he throws on.
These he's collected from a local estate
where huge white pines stand as a road-front hedge.
He raked the needle fall from the right-of-way
into a windrow of sorts, then drew a large carton along
boxing it up to re-spread at home.

The needles will keep the leaves
from flying away in autumn winds
until rain and freezes and snows
settle them, a dense weed barrier
and soil builder, the needles adding
a little acid to the mix.
In the coming summer he will often be on his knees

in the rich mulch, picking berries
from the under-story by the gallon.

He's done this all the years of marriage
and widowhood, a rotund figure
with a sharp tongue, whose ritual
is the town's ritual, whose berries
become the town's berries
as he gives away his wife's favorite,
which he will eat few of.

HORSESHOEING

My horse, these late fall mornings,
finds the first small V of sunlight,
like décolletage between the hills,
where it falls in the far corner
of the pasture.
The horse is illuminated,
warmed, before the ground
as the trees seem to wick
the sunlight over the world
in a slowly extended burn.

The farrier is due, like winter,
so my horse will be caulk-shod
for winter work.
               I keep hoof walls,
soles, and frogs trimmed
the three seasons my horse
goes barefoot, and do not mind
the smelly work with knife,
nippers, rasp, but do not want
to fit or nail a shoe.

He'll put the anvil on the tailgate
and light his small gas furnace
to modify the ordinary kegshoes
common now. The front ones he'll heat
and slap on the bottom of the hoof
to burn a proper seat and check
for fit after he's altered it
by pounding over the sharp,
rounded bickern. Two white back hooves

mean likely quarter cracks
so he'll mount bar shoes
he makes each year.
Out comes the anvil devil,
sharp piece for cutting stock.
He fits it in the hardy hole;
heats the bar stock; cuts it
quickly with heavy hammer
over the devil; reheats the cut piece
along with the shoe,
and forge welds the bar
across the tail ends,
then while they're almost red
hot fits these
to the prepared hoof.

Before he nails any in place,
he forms caulks on each shoe
with a boron rod melted
by an acetylene torch.
Boron's brilliant crystals
are especially hard and grippy.
Four caulks to each shoe
and all must be even.

I'll hold and talk to my horse
so in the tedium of repetition
she won't get antsy.
The farrier and I both
don't want him to quicken her.
Each nail must be driven
high enough in the hoof wall
to hold without breaking,

but not so high as to nick
the tender white line
which would make her lame
until he or I removed
the offending nail.
It can happen to the best.
He's only done it once
on my horses.

Done,
She'll be ready to pull
the occasional log I'll draw,
and more likely the sleigh.
The weight of the shoes
will make her lift her feet higher,
and parking out in that pretty way
we'll clip along at a good speed.
I bought the sleigh
from the daughter of the drunk
who owned it. It wears
a metal tag
from my great-grandfather's store.
I'd like to say
she'll pull me a century back,
that time is circular,
or science tells us it's all
happening at once
and we put it in linear form.
But any path to or through
the past is an icy road,
whatever the pace,
distorted by speed.

QUEBEC CITY BOARDWALK

My wife and I stood on the boardwalk,
long as a great ship's deck,
high over the St. Lawrence;
hung our heads and arms
over the wrought-iron railings
and listened to a man play a hurdy gurdy.
He held it like a fat violin
in his lap as he cranked with one hand
and pushed the keys to play
the melody strings with the other.
He played songs haunting enough
to bring the night faster—look down
at his hands as they cast daylight
shadows, look up and night pressed
around streetlamp halos.
We looked down to where small hotels
back up to the bluff the city walls
stand on. They and the shops were fed
a steady stream of customers
by the funicular cars rising and lowering
near us, and the ferry crossing
the rapid narrows.
We watched them and then followed
the river with our eyes out toward where
we drove along it during the day.
We'd walked among fifty thousand
snow geese in the fields at Cap Tormente,
then watched them in shore mire
and on littoral tidal bars
burying their heads entire
to find the rush roots they live on.

The grit was already wearing off
the reddish iron deposited
on their facial feathers by their digging
in the mineral rich far north.
The atonal honking was like a brass band
playing Schoenberg or Cage,
and their watery muttering
was like a music hall crowd murmuring
as the lights go down.
But the light had been bright
this fall day, and the murmur constant.

We'd driven on up the North Shore
and crossed many rivers falling
off the interior shield rebounding
from the weight of the last ice age,
till we came to the mouth of the Saguenay
where the highway each side
connects to ferry docks.
We thrilled at the sight of Beluga whales
feeding, and walked out to a point
away from the soft roar of traffic and ferry.

When the ferry noise subsided,
even infra-bass notes sensed not heard,
we could hear the low trill
of the white whales, also named sea canaries
for their tremulous calls
emitted as they surface.
Here, on or near the surface,
they fed on schools of smelt,
which will breed in the brackish zone
but not beyond tidal;

and spent-spawner salmon, or kelts,
that ran upriver in spring
but only now egg- and sperm- emptied
return to the sea and become prey here;
as do the yellow eels now turned
silver, who will even crawl
through damp grass and rushes
in their push to migrate back
to sea from tributaries
they matured in,
and now also become feed
for the pods of belugas that roll
and roil like white caps
in the confluence
near where the long flowing Labrador Current
hits an underwater wall
of the ancient granite shield
causing a great upwelling
in which all can feast,
and *les baleines,* no longer hunted
themselves in the great numbers
of earlier centuries, including the one
in which we were born, moved in close
to shore for even the crustaceans
carried up from the deep.
All the long drive back to the city
the wind coming in the open window
was like one exhaled breath.

We could hear the hurdy gurdy,
the drone strings first, like a bell's
constant echo in a well,
then the finicky trompettes

and finally we could discern the quick fingers
of the viellist keying the melody strings
before we topped the stairway
to the boardwalk laid out
from the bastion walls to below
the turrets of the Victorian hotel.
He held the crowd—most had never heard
or seen the like of instrument.
When he called out "Chanson des Baleines,"
we both gave a start
and pushed in closer
but after a time drew back.

In this polyphony of built
and building; architecture and history;
children's present play; the tones
of barter from the art alley;
the heartbeat-like *clop clop*
of hoof beats and the spark and grind
of iron rims on stone
from horses pulling calèches;
restaurateurs softly calling their fares,
the quiet rumble of our hunger,
becomes basic, one note of
the *cantus firmus:*
the low sound of river water
pushing through the Quebec narrows
as at the fjord-like mouth of the Sagueney;
the deep quaver of goose calls
in the feeding banks and bars.
The drone note of the *vielle à roué*
against the rosined wheel,
persisting amidst the quavery, keyed *chanterelles,*

and even with the counterpoint of ferry horn,
can seem tireless, and tiresome,
but the unmeasured plainchant
of these ordinary wonders
plays on.

LAST FISH

On a ridged corner
overlooking the highest falls
in this stream's reach,
a jumble of fir and spruce boles
have been cast outward
as if an explosion had dropped them
like jack straws.
Their root-fan bases, pried
off now bare rock, hold earth
burned to black ash. Lightning
had cleared that house-sized overlook,
its furniture cleaved and leaning
against mist-sprayed walls,
and ready to tumble.
I cast to the head of the pool the logs
would soon jam into and dam
for a time, until spring freshets.
Spawn-run brook trout rested
that day in the tail-ends of pools
under water-herded leaves.
Their sides, as colorful, would flash
as they struck my fly
from where they were maybe born,
from where their ancestors
were glacially borne.
In their world
I am lightning.

SINGLE STONE

Only steps from a cellar hole
that was the basement of his life,
now filled with saplings,
the child's grave lies amid stone wall rubble
and larger trees. A small burial
in a neighboring tree line
of someone unknown to me,
or known only by name and dates
made readable as I clear lichen
from the letters and numbers.
I also clear the vines, roots, encroaching canes
from the short mound,
just because it needs doing,
 just needs.

GATHERING

Flocking crows in a rotted elm,
if five is enough to call it flocking,
for short flight south, the year is old,
or down from the north with its harder cold
that strikes here when the wind blows through.
I stand still when I see them.
The angular stances, cock-eyed stares,
suggest I've intruded on a day of theirs,
though it couldn't belong to quite so few.
As the scavengers settle or flap and watch for loss,
their wings shine even in the late dull light,
and thus they become this iron day's gloss,
and gloss.

THREATENING WINTER

When I was a boy a jet fighter fell
out of the sky less than a mile from home.
The pilot flew because of warnings
from Thule in the long cold
that threatened a winter
we did not even know about.
When the engine was stricken
and failed the pilot bailed
and parachuted into an elderly couple's
pasture. He showed up at their door
badly burned. They drove him
to the local hospital in their Lark.
He told the couple his name
but asked them not to tell,
they didn't know if from shame
or secrecy.
                    The Air Force, who came
in great trucks with heavy equipment
to excavate the crater, announced
in local radio spots that all souvenirs
must be returned.
                    So our school bus,
a woman's station wagon hired
by the town, stopped one morning
so an eighth-grade boy could toss
the car-trunk sized piece
of aluminum fuselage skin
we'd been sitting tightly with
onto the truck bed already piled
with landing gear, wing tips,
ailerons, unrecognizable fragments,

and a muddy canopy
from a neighbor's barn yard
where it had struck, but not killed,
his best bull. Luck of some sort.
Another boy's parents made him
return a machine gun barrel,
but he kept a few rounds.

He'd used to ride his St. Bernard
to school,
   would sic him on us,
one girl badly chewed.
The town Selectmen had the dog put down;
buried him up in my uncle's field
for some reason.
     Boy said
he was going to get a functioning gun
and deal with those
who'd cost him his dog.

My family had been drawn out
that night by an odd whine
we couldn't locate till we saw
the flash rise beside the road
to a nearby pond.
    The lower sky
turned red, like when our upper
neighbor's house and barn burned,
or like when my grandparent's house
and barn burned, or when our lower
neighbor's barn burned,
or how it might have looked
out my own window if I'd risen

to watch our own barn burn,
but this flash was followed
seconds later by a clap
that would have put an end to thunder,
and, as with lightning,
we could estimate the distance
and began to walk the road toward it.
Rockets were part of the armament
we later learned,
                and local men
brought back examples they'd collected
as the Air Force gleaned
as much as it could before hard winter
set in.
Snow soon covered the crater.
The pilot almost fully recovered.

We recovered bolts and pieces of skin
and frame for years as we hunted
or fished in the area
where we hoped it likely
nothing else would fall.

HORSE FAIR

Last of the season,
and no weight pulling here—
the summer and early fall circuit
followed by most
of those present,
where cement-block-laden
stone boats are the test—
just in-hand classes
and handling displays:
singles drawing carts;
spans, unicorn hitches,
fours and sixes in hand,
pulling wagons and drays
around the village center.
After stiff driving classes
the horses' hot breath feels
and sounds like a blacksmith's
tuyered bellows.
A well kept lawn is being dented
by the hooves of a huge
dappled grey mare held
lightly on a slack lead.
The old man I'm with asks
her name. Babe is in foal
but not heavy with it.
She's led out into the largest class
with Belgians, Clydesdales,
other Percherons, Punches,
Shires, and hybrid Chunks,
such as have pulled
deep-set ploughs, combines,

haying implements,
and record loads of timber
as logs or lumber.
On this autumn common
it's show classes and confirmation
and high stepping like in a county fair day's
grand cavalcade.
                    The mare's look
and park trot earn her the overall prize.
"Prepped and shod," the judge says,
"She'd take any great Midwest state fair
confirmation class I've ribboned."
The class ends in hubbub
of horses and crowd.

"Just like the Bonheur painting,"
the old man appraises.

I've seen *The Horse Fair,*
as has he, whose father's employer
wanted the painting
when his Vanderbilt grandfather
gave it to the Met.
The father came north to the borderlands
with his rich gentleman
each summer for horse trading.
The milling of teams
at a big horse pull can seem similar
to those earlier sales events,
but now it's harness work and sweat
till stumped by the load.
Today the town's horse fair is surrounded
by steeple, school, dying general store,

and many a clapboard façade
that have stood longer
than most states have been in the union.
In the restless push for progress
such buildings have often been pulled
from foundations to roll whole
to new locations by such haunches
as grace the common.
Not like the L'Hopital Saltpietre—
in the far background of the huge canvas—
that has stood centuries on the site
of the gunpowder factory,
which invention or adoption
ended the introductory role of the horses
being escorted down the Boulevard.
On the off side of the painting
an Ardennes—"A fine beast
for war," said Caesar, who faced
its ancestors whose deep red coats
splotched with grey
echoed the dried blood and frost
from northern battles.
—hardly notices a smaller horse,
a courser to the destrier,
has cast its rider and runs amok
in the midst of the cavalcade.
One horse in back, already charged past,
puts up a fight two men can barely handle.
In the middle ground a black rears high,
his rider's arms flung high,
out of contact, out of balance.
Just beyond, beside, a pure white charger
also rears. Already on a short rein,

it strains against a strained handler
as it tries to turn and bite its rival.
Off to the right the pony of a boy
is jumping, all four feet off the ground,
and likely to buck when it lands,
the boy is in trouble.
Closest to the viewer,
two great Percherons,
looking like Babe,
white and heavily grey-dappled,
have been asked by the rider astride
one to "Trot on." He has noticed
the building furor but still holds
them lightly reined. They have arched
their necks in unison and each pushes
off strongly with one rear leg
and brings the other forward
while the opposite foreleg snaps high
for the rapid and stylish advance
with cold-blooded calm
noted of the breed,
not the skittish plunge
of the warm-blood heating the scene.
The whole flow to the upper tree-lined,
spectator-lined, promanade
of equines is disrupted
under a roiled, disrupted sky
still filled with shadowing sunlight.

Those steeds stood then at the height
of their usefulness. More heavily muscled
even than those that carried
a knight into battle, a single example

of the great horse progeny
could turn more soil in an hour
than ten men might till in a day;
could pull more stores or wares
than any number of hand carts
or barrows, though those work horses
died in such numbers on city streets
it often smelled like an army
had lost a great battle.

Babe's owner is in earnest,
works her hard sugaring,
haying, reaping, logging,
but she lives out of time:
A day late and a dollar short.
A day after the fair.

Beyond the village this autumn
color-spangled day, this autumn harvest day,
tractors taller than a mounted knight's head
trundle across fields, down highways,
each reaping and ferrying such riches
as a grand caravan might
have been able to haul.

Today a pony gets away
from his lovely little master,
and she runs after.
Leads and lounge lines tighten
and shod and unshod hooves go flying
all along this wide Main street.
The old man I'm with yells
to the girl "Stand still,"

but she doesn't understand
how the pony will likely return
to the hand that feeds it.

In myriad connections,
cells and synapses are creating
a scene as seeming solid as a painting,
so fleeting muddle will stand still,
to be recreated entire as haunt or joy,
bidden or unbidden,
in the future's ever just-past present.

DEER CAMP

The drive in is long
over bad logging roads gone worse.
The camp sits on a wooded point
reaching into the marsh that stretches far
to the south, forming a bowl
amid the surrounding hills.
Those dozen miles of hardwood ridgelines
falling off to softwoods
are perfect for feeding whitetail,
which also come down to drink from springs
and runs in the drainage.

Before first light the ground and cover
creaked and snapped with each footfall
so I stayed on stand
as the ridge seemed to rise into sunlight.
The early frost dissipated,
the leaves and wood grasses softened.

Almost every fall our grade school teacher's husband
would pull into the school yard
and the dozen-and-a-half students
of all eight grades would troop out
to admire the buck roped across
the fender of some big Buick.

My grandfather seldom got a deer
but would tell at day's end
of the streams he'd followed
to source-end springs; the wooded vales
he'd crossed; the climb to the top

of new-forested hills, clear cut
before his youth for sheep pasture,
from which he could once see his world.

Before I head up the ridge
I follow a game trail out
to overgrown pastures
with apple trees and wolf trees
in the edges.
When my father-in-law disembarked
on Seabee built docks
to go to war in France
he remembers villagers
passing him Calvados
in a jar he declined to share
with fellow soldiers.
                        He vaguely remembers
stretches of browned rich pastures,
and bare apple trees whose fruit had been pressed
and distilled for the fine cider brandy
that made the day's march easy
through territory reminding him of home,
the hedgerows like stone-walled tree lines.

I skirted along abandoned stone walls,
then headed up toward deer's mid-day cover.
Several hours of stalking later
a deer, put up on a small plateau,
leapt off over blackberry canes and slash.
                    I ducked around the side hill
        to keep the quartering wind
at an angle between us.
I saw him next side-on

in over-browsed firs.
The shot allowed a half leap
                    and the terrible tumble
when the soft thud ended the heart's work.

Sleeves rolled high in the cold,
I sliced and pulled, and reached high
in the new cavity to remove liver,
lights, and ruptured heart.
I would even sever the tongue
in the final cut up,
not wanting to waste
a thing from this toll.

I roped the head by the antlers
to my waist and began
the long drag.

The great bog lay before me
as I angled off the ridge.
Lost in a snowstorm on that same ridge,
my father-in-law faced what he knew
was a northwest wind
all the way down to a logging road
that led by camp. He was as white
as the weather-side of the trees,
snow lodged in every clothing crevice,
and was driven so hard
it was sometimes hard to breathe.
    It didn't seem so much.
                A new recruit
in a bloodied regiment, unknown,
not knowing anyone he had lain with

in a brush hut
the size of our deer camp
in the Hürtgen Forest in a driving snow
with tree bursts from shelling
shattering all around,
driving wood-chip shrapnel
down so digging down was no protection.
              The next day was Kesternich,
village fighting on the way to the Rhine,
scrabbling over stones
that had been the houses,
crawling under tight drifts of rusted wire,
all the time under fire.
He said the German machine guns were better,
sounded like a telephone book ripping.
He carried three boxes of machine gun shells,
then two, then one, then the gun itself
as all of his squad but him were undone,
remnants shifted from one company to another.
The 2nd Lieutenant shot one of his own men
running away
            before he himself was done for.
As my father-in-law bent in a crater,
shrapnel the size of his thumb ripped
open his leg, tore through his knee
and he couldn't operate the gun or himself.
            When he woke in the dark,
he hoped of the same day,
he could only move by pushing
himself backwards on his ass
with the busted barrel of a carbine.
He scraped himself over rubble,
everything covered with a dust

like gun powder,
               and back under the wire,
though repeatedly caught and exhausted,
till by daybreak he pushed himself against
a machine gun nest where he didn't know
the day's new password.
                         But they took his word
and carried him back to the aid station.
Months in a body cast followed,
                     with a bar between his knees
like a big satchel handle. His knee
wouldn't bend when the plaster was removed,
but a doctor and two male nurses grabbed
him and the leg, and broke
the scar tissue and calcium spurs
with an excruciating wrench
that he says sounded like rifle fire.

               He and eight others,
home from war, went out of their way
to get away to this cut over land,
and stayed the next hunting season
in a defunct logging
camp called Bear's Den,
long since collapsed.
Long vistas back then.
Feeding deer could be seen for a mile.
They got two and strapped
them on the fenders of a '32 Ford
with an engine almost ruined
by kerosene in the war.
They found out forty acres were for sale
and bought them together,

each and all whole owners.

When I draw into camp
he helps me hang the carcass
above the possible night visit of coyotes,
and to let in cure.
Spruce, fir, and birches hem
the clearing pretty tightly.

All these years later, the camp he built,
crude and small, sitting in the middle
of a regrown forest, at the edge
of a startling bog,
                    still has the feel
of a retreat from war;
                      the only place
he will talk about it,
                  the only one
left he knew who can.

FELLING THE ELM

Not the last one on the street—
water shoots from old stumps
line a field-drain swale farther on—
but the largest, and dying
before leaf change, great branches
of leaves browning
like sandy grass hummocks
in summer swelter.

In my youth I drew hay
to my grandmother's barn
down this same street
then overarched by elm boughs.
Glorious to ride in shade
after the sweat of the open field.

I notch the pasture side
where I've moved the fence
for a clear fall away from the house.
The chain saw races in; I stop
and drive a wedge behind
to assure direction. My horse races
along the far fence
as the tree knuckles and crashes.

I planted the elm the year of our son's birth.
Ordered from hybridizers who, trying to save
the species, grew
scions back-crossed six times
against disease, it stood
as testament; now falls that way,
resistant, but not immune.

WRAPPING THE PEARS

Pears will blet if left to tree ripen
so I've picked them early.
I cut newspaper across the grain
and ripped neat squares along it
so the fairly soft paper
would cradle each fruit
I carefully wrapped.
I only store them two or three layers deep,
easily bruised, my work
would be for even less
if weight or handling mar them.
Over the season's course
my small crop becomes expensive,
and the tall narrow trees
make them harder to pick than apples.
One year I tried taping bottles
over some blossoms
for the fruit-in-bottle trick
of some French perry.
I filled them with fermented juice
and placed them in cool storage.
My wife told me coolly on tasting
I needn't offer her such a drink again.
But the carefully boxed pears
will ripen in two weeks,
softening to that juicy texture
with stone cell grit that defines them,
the warmer season distilled
in a peak of perfection
and quick decay.

LIMING LILACS AND CLEMATIS

Soil sours.
Ours born from exfoliation,
glacier grind, rock flour,
and humus just since the ice age,
and laying under a cold wet climate
and the wear it produces,
leaches soluble alkaloids,
called sweetness,
that many plants require.
Some, like sphagnum in the swamps,
blueberries on the uplands,
need acid soil, born
where they and such thin soils
were borne by ice, wind, water.
Lilacs seem age old here
by doorway and cellar hole,
but arrived from temperate Asia.
Clematis are native, but garden hybrids
arrived with immigrants
carrying living memories with them.
Every fall I lime my Syringa hedge
and my fence line of overreaching clematis.
I also lime the huge lilac bush
at my parents', and the single straggling jackmani,
which struggles at that altitude.
I run a soil test every third or fourth year–
some comfort to know
that in my life
I can measure
some small sweetness.

GRAPE ARBOR

The Concord grapes that overarch
the arbor; grow into the willow;
almost hide the gable
of our house, are native
to the continent, at least
the vines they were bred from.
Picking the large clumps
of fruit stains my skin
and clothes, and the splatter
when simmering for juice, purée, or pies
stains floors, counters, and utensils,
but for the taste like sweet soil
and honey combined
I bear it.
    Concord grape was the first
juice bottled, proving Pasteur's method
of boiling would preserve.
Methodists and my teetotaling
Presbyterian ancestors that bought
Mr. Welch's product
called it unfermented wine,
no transubstantiation,
no fermentation,
no kneeling—standing
to face God in his image—
no new miracles or saints,
the age of miracles past
though not the age of wonders.

My family and I drink the juice
with our worldly breakfast.

I've trimmed the vines
that would delimb the trees
as easily as a great bull elephant
pulling down food
if I let them.

In our time we've come to have
more accurate measures than Man,
but the standards are often small,
machine read at tiny distances.
Some would have us combine
the mechanical, electronic,
and human knowledge to replace us.
We've all tasted canned goods,
necessary foods in tin plate
like what sat in line camps;
lined the holds of ships
exploring the polar regions;
made seasonal and distant crops
a year round affair.
We also know the compromise.
My simple plea would be
let's not can man.
I want my children to live long,
but also to die.
Let the energy we encumber
once again take flight,
become photons,
plant-nourishing,
wonder-illuminating,
universe-spanning light.

RISING DAMP

Rotting bricks at the chimney base
will bring the whole thing down,
a thudding sudden collapse through the middle of the house,
if I don't replace them.
One by one I chip them out.
Rising damp from the later-poured concrete floor
around the base has softened the old clay
and grout. The hammer drives the chisel
deep into faulty ones. They thunk.
Healthy ones ring with such a rap.
One out, one in is the process,
maybe two in places. I set new, harder bricks
and grout them in with mortar slackened
with lime like the former.
Modern mortar would break the surrounding old ones
if not softened.

My uncle, a sometime mason, once had to drop
an entire chimney down its own throat.
It rose three stories through the middle of a mansion with
plastered walls and closets on every side.
He stood on existing chimney and knocked
the bricks down. Dust and creosote
from coal and clay rose in a cloud like smoke
around him as he worked his way down.
He used the clean-out door at the base
to clear the rubble, up and down the ladder
and cellar stairs time and again
till the shaft was clear, then clear down.
He had to build the chimney up again from the inside out.
I could not have stood

within the shaft, and had those cast concrete blocks
lowered around me, just able to fit through,
and set them on the mortar I'd trowelled
as I stood on a thin metal step placed the day before
on that days drying work. He could only work
to the height of his up-stretched arms each day,
almost fully cased by then, till his helper hauled
him up with the small windlass
used to lower the chimney blocks.
Lazarus was not brave, just lucky.
I can only do one or two bricks at a time each day.
Even here creosote or coal oil from the old furnace
has run down and stained the brick face.
What a fire that would feed, what a leveling flame.
My uncle said his was hot work.
I don't even break a sweat.

The same uncle said recently about a blue suit,
"I bought it to be laid out in;
now I'm wearing it to the wakes of others.
Life takes so long."
Wear.

TO OUR VERMONT FATHER ON HIS EARLY WINTER BIRTHDAY

Our father who is in hospital,
hallowed be your name
though you are hollowed.
Your kingdom gone,
your will undone
on this earth, and there is no heaven.
You gave us, until this day, our daily bread,
and you forgave us our debts,
though you could not forgive your other debtors.
A fierce Scot, you were not led into temptation,
and tried to deliver us from evil.
You worked your life in the Northeast Kingdom
with power,
and no glory,
ever.

Winter Ready was typeset in Dante, which was designed from 1946 to 1954 by Giovanni Mardersteig at the Officina Bodoni, as the press returned to full production after the Second World War. Mardersteig's goal was to create a new book face type with an italic face that worked seamlessly and elegantly with the roman. The designer was meticulous about detail, and he continued refining Dante for years.

Dante was the last and final type that Mardersteig designed, as well as one of his finest. The name comes from an edition of *Trattatello in laude di Dante* by Boccaccio—the first book to use Dante—which was published at the Officina Bodoni in 1955, the year that the Monotype Corporation of London issued the typeface for machine composition.

The new digital version of Dante, redrawn by Monotype's Ron Carpenter, is free from any restrictions imposed by hot metal technology. In 1993, Dante was issued in a range of three weights with a set of titling capitals, which are used for page titles or headings.

∾

PRINTED BY SPC MARCOM
SPRINGFIELD, VERMONT

TYPOGRAPHY & DESIGN
BY DEDE CUMMINGS
BRATTLEBORO, VERMONT